the introvert journal for teens

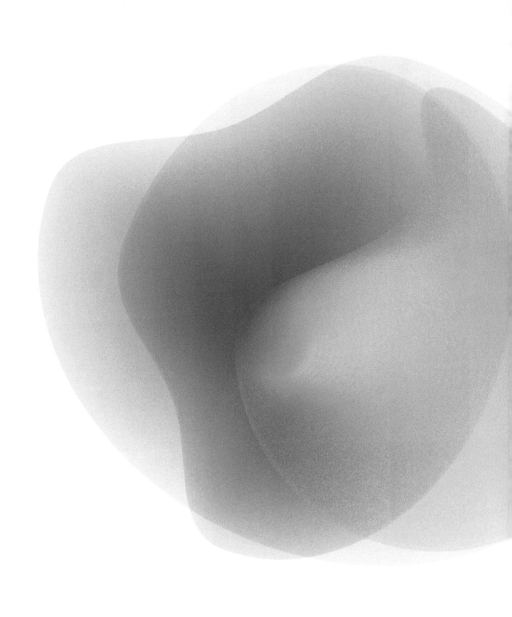

the introvert journal *for teens*

Guided Prompts to Help You Navigate Life and Celebrate Your Quiet Strengths

Jessika Fruchter, LMFT

ROCKRIDGE
PRESS

For general information on our other products and services or to obtain technical support, please contact our Customer Care Department within the United States at (866) 744-2665, or outside the United States at (510) 253-0500.

Rockridge Press publishes its books in a variety of electronic and print formats. Some content that appears in print may not be available in electronic books, and vice versa.

TRADEMARKS: Rockridge Press and the Rockridge Press logo are trademarks or registered trademarks of Callisto Media Inc. and/or its affiliates, in the United States and other countries, and may not be used without written permission. All other trademarks are the property of their respective owners. Rockridge Press is not associated with any product or vendor mentioned in this book.

Interior and Cover Designer: Francesca Pacchini
Art Producer: Sara Feinstein
Editor: Nora Spiegel
Production Editor: Jenna Dutton
Production Manager: Riley Hoffman

Illustrations used under license from Diana Hlevnjak / Polar Vectors.

Paperback ISBN: 978-1-64876-557-5

R0

this journal belongs to:

Sophia ♡

To all the young people I have worked with throughout the years. Your breadth of insight, creativity, and resilience has been nothing short of an inspiration.

contents

Introduction

Welcome! I'm so glad you've found your way here.

My name is Jessika Fruchter, and I'm a licensed psychotherapist and expressive arts therapist. I'm also a proud introvert who picked up her first journal at the age of 13 and never stopped writing.

For nearly a decade, I've supported teens like you as they've learned to navigate an extroverted world. By working with this journal, you're beginning an important journey to embrace your quiet power. These pages are filled with bite-size pieces of wisdom, knowledge, and creative actions you can take to grow more fully into yourself and navigate the world on your own terms.

What Does It Mean to Be an Introvert?

Good question! First off, let's talk a little history. In the 1920s, psychologist Carl Jung was one of the first to define the personality types of introversion and extroversion. Over time, the concepts made their way into popular culture, so you'll often hear people describe themselves as introverts or extroverts. However, it's important to know that there is no one kind of introvert or extrovert; everyone has their own unique personality.

In general, people who are more extroverted tend to seek out large groups or louder spaces to recharge. On the opposite end of the spectrum, introverts tend to recharge in quiet spaces and prefer small groups or one-on-one social interactions. This may be because introverted people tend to be more sensitive to external stimuli like sound and light.

Neither introversion nor extroversion is better or worse than the other. They are just different. We'll talk more about traits of introverts in the next section. Introverts, however, do face unique challenges, as they are regularly navigating an extroverted world.

Here's an example: In many American high-school classrooms, students will be rewarded for behaviors that are often challenging for more introverted teens (such as raising your hand and speaking) and may lose points for being too quiet or for daydreaming—behaviors that are more natural and beneficial for introverts. As you move through the sections in this journal, you'll learn new ways to navigate challenges like these and to live your best introverted life.

You May Be an Introvert If . . .

- Your idea of a fun Friday night is a movie night with your best friend instead of a big party with people you don't really know.
- You're creative and/or artistic.
- You need a good amount of downtime to recharge after going to a large party.
- You enjoy your own company.
- Friends often come to you for insight or advice.
- Your moods shift easily depending on your environment.
- You have an active imagination and love to daydream.
- Leaving your texts unread is the norm rather than the exception.

- You often feel misunderstood by peers and adults.
- You're more likely to stand back and observe than be the center of attention.
- Quiet is your friend.
- You may feel nervous or overwhelmed in social situations.
- People mistake your quiet nature for shyness.
- Sometimes you feel anxious or overwhelmed and can't figure out why.

And It's a Good Thing You Are, Because . . .

- You have a heightened level of self-awareness. This helps you know yourself *and* how you impact others.
- Your happiness does not depend solely on interactions with others.
- You have the capacity to concentrate on things for long periods of time.
- You think things through and shy away from impulsive decisions.
- You are an empathetic friend and show up for the people you love.
- You are creative and innovative, often coming up with new ideas or works of art.
- You're self-motivated and can work independently.
- You're intuitive and know how to trust your instincts.
- You're a leader and encourage others to be their authentic selves.
- **You have quiet power!**

How to Use This Journal

While this journal is designed for teens who are more introverted, anyone can benefit from using it. Many of the exercises and writing prompts are geared toward self-exploration and self-discovery. The quotes and anecdotes featured in this book are here to offer the inspiration of others who have embraced their most authentic selves. Ultimately, that's what this journal is all about.

The journal is divided into four sections that explore themes of introversion, self-discovery, relationships, and your future self, but feel free to skip around and follow your interests. Trust your instincts here, and your process. How and when you use this journal is up to you. You may choose to set aside time each day to work on a prompt or an exercise, or you may just pick up this journal when you are craving some time for reflection or creativity.

No matter how you choose to move forward on this journey, I hope you'll do so with curiosity and joy!

section I
We're All a Little Different

As an introvert, one of your superpowers is self-knowledge, and you're always learning, growing, and changing. The first section of this journal includes writing prompts designed to help you unpack your unique experience of introversion and exercises that will help you deepen your understanding of yourself through art and conversation. Also included are skills-based practices to support you in taking care of yourself as you better learn how to navigate an extroverted world.

Find out who you are and do it on purpose.

—DOLLY PARTON, country music singer-songwriter

Maybe you were the person at school who preferred to read alone at lunchtime, or who longed to escape from big, loud family dinners at home. What are the earliest messages you received about your need for quiet and/or alone time? Did you feel supported and understood? Did you feel pressured to socialize when you didn't want to? Think about the messages you may have received as a kid that you still hold close, and journal about them.

- "Always treat people the way you want to be treated"

- "Only have elevator friends"

- "Make the days count"

- "It's not what you say, it's how you say it."

What are your superpowers? Everyone has them, and they're the gifts that are unique to us. Are you empathetic or insightful? Maybe you are creative or a leader? Take a moment to make a list or write down notes about your personal superpowers.

- Empathetic
- Up-stander
- Strong leader.
- Good friend
- Kind
- Helpful
- Smart
- Good Student

Inside/Outside Mask

Some people act confident when they are really feeling anxious or uncertain. Others smile when they are actually feeling sad. What parts do you show the world? What parts do you tuck away? Let's make an "inside/outside" mask representing the parts of yourself that you show the world and the parts that you keep private. To create the mask, draw the outline of a face on a blank piece of paper and cut it out. On one side, draw or collage a representation of the parts you show the world—in other words, your public face. Turn it over and draw or collage your private face.

What would these two faces say to each other if they were having a conversation?

_____

_____

_____

_____

_____

_____

_____

Positive affirmations highlight our own strengths, abilities, and intentions. We often use them to challenge negative or unhelpful thoughts. You'll often see them floating around social media as memes with phrases like "I am beautiful," "I am strong," "I am capable," and "I am loved." Write 10 to 20 positive affirmations that would help you disarm your negative thoughts. Choose affirmations that feel believable to you.

_____

_____

_____

_____

_____

_____

_____

_____

_____

_____

_____

_____

Rosa Parks, CIVIL RIGHTS ACTIVIST

Civil rights activist Rosa Parks reminds us that quiet courage can change the course of history. It was the evening of December 1, 1955, when Ms. Parks, a Black woman living in Montgomery, Alabama, refused to give up her seat to a white passenger on a segregated bus. At that time, segregation of Black people was commonplace, and Ms. Parks was tired of the injustice she and so many others endured. While Ms. Parks was said to be introverted with a soft voice, her bold action that evening set in motion a yearlong boycott of the Montgomery busing system and later launched a national effort to end racial segregation in public spaces. Her heroism illustrates calm resistance.

Bullying occurs in many different forms, from explicit verbal jabs to threatening body language. You may have experienced this yourself, or perhaps you know others who have. Maybe you've even been the bully. Think about an experience you've had related to bullying. What happened? How do you think this experience has impacted your feelings about yourself? What did you learn?

_____

_____

_____

_____

_____

_____

_____

_____

_____

_____

_____

_____

_____

_____

_____

_____

Being an introvert doesn't mean you're shy. It means you enjoy being alone. Not just enjoy it—you need it.

—AMY SCHUMER, comedian and actress

It's common to compare yourself to others from time to time, but it's not always helpful. Who in your life do you admire, and who do you compare yourself to? They could be friends and family members or celebrities and influencers. How do you think this comparison helps or harms you?

_____

_____

_____

_____

_____

_____

_____

_____

_____

_____

_____

_____

_____

_____

Practice Self-Compassion

Are you your own toughest critic? So many of us are. Self-criticism often presents with thoughts like *I should have done better* or *I am not* _____ *enough*. Let's practice self-compassion as a way to ease that harsh inner voice. For today, when you notice harsh or judgy thoughts, instead of trying to change them or push them away, offer a counter thought that is kind. Perhaps it could be something you would say to a friend. If one full day feels like too much, try just one hour.

Here's an example:

Self-critical thought: *I should have gotten A's in every class.*

Self-compassionate thought: *I work hard in all my classes and that is enough.*

What feelings arose when you countered self-critical thoughts with self-compassion? Did it come naturally, or did it feel challenging?

_____

_____

_____

_____

_____

Self-Care One Day at a Time

Self-care can mean different things to different people, but at its core, self-care is about tending to our unique personality and needs. Try to commit to integrating one self-care practice into your schedule this week. It could be a neighborhood walk, giving yourself extra quiet time, or an arts practice—whatever feels enjoyable to you. Next, schedule it and ask a family member or friend to support you in taking good care of yourself.

We all get tongue-tied from time to time. In fact, introverts report this as a common experience during large social gatherings or when talking to new people. Write about a time when you struggled to know what to say or you just felt uncomfortable saying it. Looking back now, what about the situation made you feel tongue-tied, and what, if anything, would you do differently in the future?

_____

_____

_____

_____

_____

_____

_____

_____

_____

_____

_____

_____

_____

_____

Abstract Self-Portrait

Let's explore your complex identity by creating an abstract self-portrait. An abstract self-portrait is different from a literal self-portrait. In an abstract self-portrait, you may use symbols, colors, textures, words, and shapes to represent aspects of yourself instead of creating a literal drawing of yourself. Look at the abstract portraits of Pablo Picasso or Jean-Michel Basquiat for inspiration. You can use whatever art materials you have available, such as pencils, watercolors, markers, paint, and paper.

Challenges can be uncomfortable, but they can also be opportunities for growth. We may try to avoid them, but naming them and embracing the experience can go a long way toward better understanding ourselves. Let's explore areas of growth. Begin by finishing this sentence: *The hardest thing for me is* _____. Fill in the blank with whatever words come to mind and repeat the sentence as many times as you like.

_____

_____

_____

_____

_____

_____

_____

_____

_____

_____

_____

_____

_____

Have you ever felt misunderstood? Our quietness can be confused for shyness, and our tendency to get lost in our thoughts can be confused for zoning out. If you've ever felt misunderstood, this is an opportunity to share your thoughts, feelings, and frustrations. Try completing this sentence: *If you only knew* _____. Fill in the blank with your thoughts, such as *If you only knew how scared I am sometimes* or *If you only knew my strength*. What do you want to be known about you? Repeat this as many times as you want.

_____

_____

_____

_____

_____

_____

_____

_____

_____

_____

_____

_____

_____

Planned Daydreaming

Daydreaming often gets a bad rap as a waste of time. I disagree wholeheartedly! Set aside time to intentionally turn yourself inward and see what comes to mind. Set a timer for 30 to 60 minutes and get comfortable. What ideas or visions stir in your imagination? What do you find yourself thinking about? Next, make a collage based on what came to mind. A sheet of paper or piece of cardboard can be your canvas, and you'll need a glue stick and images from magazines, catalogs, or photos. You can use scissors to cut out the images, or tear them out for a less precise look. Did anything about this process surprise you?

How comfortable do you feel saying no when someone asks you to do something you don't want to do? Boundaries are part of every healthy relationship, but we can feel guilt or shame about setting them for fear of disappointing others. Introverts often feel pressured to attend social events or agree to favors when they would rather spend time on their own. Reflect on a time when you experienced a similar pressure. What happened, and how did you feel? Looking back, would you respond differently?

_____

_____

_____

_____

_____

_____

_____

_____

_____

_____

_____

_____

_____

Alessia Cara, SINGER-SONGWRITER

Alessia Cara is a singer and songwriter who channeled her own experience as a teenage introvert into the global hit song "Here." Cara's lyrics tell the story of her attending a party and wondering why she had gone when she didn't want to be there. The sentiments expressed in the song are common among introverts, who frequently feel more comfortable on their own or in small groups. The media has frequently pointed to the song as an unofficial anthem for introverts. "People turned it into this song that speaks for a demographic that doesn't have a voice, like introverts," she told *Billboard* magazine in December 2016.

One of the hallmarks of introversion is the need for downtime, but like everyone else, we also crave connection and time with people we care about. Take a moment to reflect on how you know when you need self-care to recharge. What are the cues? Do you get irritable or tired? Do you start to space out? Journal about it in the space below.

_____

_____

_____

_____

_____

_____

_____

_____

_____

_____

_____

_____

_____

_____

_____

Postcards Never Sent

As introverts, we may have much to say, but we don't always feel comfortable saying it. Still, it can be helpful to have an outlet so we don't bottle everything inside. As a release for these unspoken thoughts, we can create "Postcards Never Sent." Using index cards, note cards, or paper, you can draw on one side of the card and write a message on the other for someone to whom you have something to express. These can be as simple or elaborate as you like. When you're finished, you may put the postcards away for safekeeping or discard them. The idea is to externalize your thoughts and feelings in a way that feels comfortable.

All that you touch
You Change.
All that you Change
Changes you.

−OCTAVIA E. BUTLER, author of *Parable of the Sower*

Let's explore how our thoughts influence our feelings. For one full day, be extra mindful of your thoughts and track them in a way that feels manageable. This could be notes on your phone or in a notebook. After tracking your thoughts for one day, use this space to reflect on your observations without judgment. What thoughts did you have throughout the day? Did you notice themes or certain repeating thoughts? What feelings arose in connection with these thoughts?

_____

_____

_____

_____

_____

_____

_____

_____

_____

_____

_____

_____

_____

Metaphors use symbols as a way to describe and understand something else. Let's explore our identities through metaphor. What animal do you most identify with? Feel free to select more than one and use this space to explore how the animals are similar to you. What traits do you share? How do you spend your days? What strengths and challenges do you face? Now try describing yourself using the animal as a metaphor. For example, you might say, *I am a lion. Golden like the sun. I move in silence, always watching.*

_____

_____

_____

_____

_____

_____

_____

_____

_____

_____

_____

_____

_____

Meditation When You Don't Want to Meditate

Many people think of meditation as a practice that involves sitting in an uncomfortable position for long stretches of time, but did you know meditation can actually feel good? Let's try an easy meditation practice to help ground you when you're feeling overwhelmed.

1. Prepare a comfortable space to lie down—complete with blankets and pillows if you like! Alternatively, if you feel most comfortable when moving, you may choose to walk.

2. Next, set a timer for a period of time that feels realistic to you.

3. To begin, simply focus on your breathing. Notice how your belly rises and falls with each breath.

4. You may observe your mind wandering during this time, which is completely normal. Acknowledge your thought and release it. Now, gently bring your awareness back to your breathing.

5. Continue focusing on your breathing until your time is up.

What did you notice about your practice? Did this experience help calm you?

_____

_____

_____

_____

Envision Your Happy Place

Everyone experiences challenging times, and learning how to develop coping strategies in those moments is essential. This visualization is useful for when you need to increase a feeling of safety or calm. Here's how it works:

1. Sit or stand in a comfortable position and close your eyes. This is best done in a place where you won't be disturbed. You can play soothing music if that is helpful for you.

2. Then imagine yourself in a serene setting where you are safe and relaxed. It may be a white sand beach or your grandma's kitchen table. It may be a place you've been or have never been.

3. Take in the sounds and smells. What can you feel in this safe place? What do you touch? Let yourself dwell here.

4. When you are ready return, slowly open your eyes and pay attention to the outside world.

It's a common misconception that introverts don't like or need relationships, but this couldn't be further from the truth. Relationships are deeply important to us, though the way we connect may look different. Introverts, for example, may choose to have a small group of close friends or spend time engaged in more quiet activities. Use the space below to doodle or draw a visual representation of the people in your life who support you and whom you support. This may look like a web, a solar system, a chart, etc. Any format will work as long as it allows you to identify your important relationships.

Interview with an Introvert

Relationships often serve as mirrors. We can learn so much about ourselves and each other by opening up dialogue. Choose a friend or family member whom you suspect may also be an introvert and invite them to have a conversation about your shared trait. You may want to prepare questions beforehand and write them down. Perhaps you wonder about how your friend or family member handles social pressures or how they take care of themselves when they are feeling drained. The experience may push you a bit out of your comfort zone, so you could try to select someone with whom you feel comfortable.

What was it like hearing someone else's experience navigating an extroverted world? What are the similarities and differences with your experience? Did you gain any tips or insight you can apply to your own life?

_____

_____

_____

_____

_____

_____

_____

_____

_____

What or whom are you grateful for in your life? It's easy to take the small things for granted, especially when times are challenging. Practicing gratitude does not ignore the hard stuff, but it does help create a fuller picture of our lives. Take as much space here as you need to write about what you appreciate, and notice how it makes you feel.

_____

_____

_____

_____

_____

_____

_____

_____

_____

_____

_____

_____

_____

Let's think about how you can best care for yourself when you are feeling depleted from social time. Create a list or make a chart of actions you can take to care for yourself when you need to recharge. Some examples may include a nature walk, napping, meditation, making art, or cooking.

_____

_____

_____

_____

_____

_____

_____

_____

_____

_____

Date with Myself

Today you are invited to go on a special date . . . with yourself!
Maybe you'll want to take yourself to lunch and go thrifting, play
basketball, or go to a museum. Maybe your ideal day is spent with
a pen and journal in hand? Engage in activities that bring you joy.
What feelings arise when you think about these activities? Does
engaging in joyful activity feel natural, or do you tend to prioritize
other tasks?

section 2
The Real You

Our identities are complex and always evolving, especially during the teen years. In this leg of the journey, you're invited to dive deep into exploring what makes you *you*—including your interests, quirks, strengths, and challenges. Here, you'll find writing prompts to help you explore different aspects of your identity, as well as creative activities to take your exploration off the page and into the world. Expect to learn about yourself and maybe even discover something new.

The real journey is right here. The great excursion starts from exactly where you are.

—**RUMI**, 13th-century Persian poet

Get to know yourself better by exploring your many identities, traits, and interests. Begin by writing the phrase: *I am* _____. Fill in the blank with whatever words come to mind: *I am a daughter, I am quiet and strong*, or *I am misunderstood*. Repeat this as many times as you're able, uncovering the various aspects of your true self. Try not to censor yourself. Be open and truthful with yourself to understand the many dimensions of you.

_____

_____

_____

_____

_____

_____

_____

_____

_____

_____

_____

_____

_____

_____

Frida Kahlo, ARTIST

Using vivid color and evocative imagery, Frida Kahlo emerged as one of Mexico's most unique artists in the early 1900s. A well-known introvert, Kahlo created art based on her own perception of reality and was not concerned with the labels assigned by others. About one-third of her paintings were self-portraits, and Kahlo has said that she painted herself because she was often in her own company. Kahlo was a free spirit even as a child and later developed into a social activist. Still, she did not have a life without challenges. At the age of six, she contracted polio, which impaired her physical abilities, and later in adulthood, she sustained serious injuries from a streetcar accident. Kahlo was said to have used painting as a way to aid her healing process.

Your Personal Soundtrack

Ever notice how the best movies often have the best soundtracks? That's because music has the power to create and shift mood. What would the soundtrack for your life sound like? Create your own personal soundtrack focusing on a certain period of time in your past or present experience, or go big and create a soundtrack for your vision of the future! If you feel comfortable, share your playlist with someone close to you when you're finished.

List the songs you picked and the moods you associate with each one.

_____

_____

_____

_____

_____

_____

_____

_____

_____

_____

_____

_____

Here's an opportunity to brag. That's right, you read correctly—
brag! We're often told to be modest or downplay our gifts, but there
is value in truly reflecting on what you feel you're good at and what
gifts you have to offer the world, whether it's mathematics, opera
singing, or being a good friend. Try to fill the page with your gifts,
and notice what feelings come up when you are writing. Do you
feel comfortable? Are you hesitant? Do you have difficulty naming
your gifts?

_____

_____

_____

_____

_____

_____

_____

_____

_____

_____

_____

_____

Let your mind wander to your most ideal day—the best day ever. What would that day entail? Where would you be? Would you be on your own or with someone else? Write about your daydream in as much detail as possible and try not to censor yourself. Did you learn anything new about yourself? What surprised you about your vision? What didn't?

_____

_____

_____

_____

_____

_____

_____

_____

_____

_____

_____

_____

_____

_____

_____

I knew who I was
this morning, but
I've changed a few times
since then.

−**LEWIS CARROLL**, author of *Alice's Adventures in
Wonderland*

Through dreams, our minds are hard at work during the night processing our experiences, hopes, fears, passions, and more. Reflect on the messages of your dreams. Use this space to write in detail about a dream and about the feelings you had upon waking. If you find you have difficulty remembering your dreams, you may keep this journal by your bedside so you can jot down what you remember as soon as you wake up. You may also use an older dream that has left a lasting impression. Were there any elements of the dream that stood out? What would the title of the dream be if it were a piece of art? Was there a message or some wisdom conveyed in the dream?

_____

_____

_____

_____

_____

_____

_____

_____

_____

_____

_____

_____

The Life Map

Our experiences help shape and form our identity. Creating a life map allows you to take inventory of the important events that shape who you are. You'll need a sheet of paper, in any size, though if you have access to a large sheet of paper, you may prefer that. Begin by drawing a road or path on the paper. There is no wrong way to do this; it will be uniquely your own! Has your journey taken place on a winding road? A bumpy road? What material is the road made of? Has the path changed at different points? Once you've determined the geography of the road, you can begin to think of important events in your life. Maybe there's just one, or maybe there are many. Next, draw symbols or images to represent these events.

Did creating this map help you notice any patterns or themes in your life? What did you learn about yourself or your journey?

_____

_____

_____

_____

_____

Do you ever give yourself a hard time? Most of us do on occasion. Think back to a time when you've gotten caught up in self-judgment. Do you find yourself judging your appearance or personality traits? Do you get upset with yourself if you make a mistake? Complete this sentence as many times as it feels helpful to you. *I am hardest on myself when . . .*

_____

_____

_____

_____

_____

_____

_____

_____

_____

_____

_____

_____

_____

The Inner Critic

Everyone has an inner critic—that part of ourselves that voices our insecurities and self-doubt. Let's take a closer look at your inner critic so that you can better recognize and manage your insecurities. First, let's try creating what your inner critic looks like. Using any art materials you have on hand, give your inner critic a face. Then, in the space below, answer the following questions, adding in any additional information about your inner critic that comes to mind: What is your inner critic's name? Where do they live? Do they enjoy their job? If so, what motivates them? What do they need to quiet down? Keep in mind that if the answers don't come immediately, that's just fine. See what arises when you try to get to know your inner critic.

_____

_____

_____

_____

_____

On a scale of 1 to 10 (with "1" being not at all and "10" being all the time), how much does your inner critic influence your choices?

1 2 3 4 5 6 7 8 9 10

Many of us are introduced to the concept of personal values when we are very young; however, these values shift and develop over time. Try to reflect on your own core values. Use the space below to write 5 to 10 values that reflect who you are as a person. Examples might be integrity, family, justice, and kindness. Check in with yourself to confirm your answers are truly your values and not values you feel you *should* have. Now consider this: Do you live in alignment with these values? If not, what actions can you take to do so?

_____

_____

_____

_____

_____

_____

_____

_____

_____

_____

_____

_____

_____

Treat Yourself!

Here's an invitation to treat yourself! Before you do, though, let's take a moment to really tap into what would feel most nourishing. You can do this quickly:

1. First, place both feet on the ground—sitting or standing—close your eyes, and take three deep breaths.

2. Ask yourself: What is it that I need most today? What comes to mind? Shopping with your best friend? Basketball? A brownie? There are no wrong answers here.

3. If you're able to make time for this treat today, go for it! If not, practice these steps again when you have more time.

What feelings or thoughts arose as you explored your needs? What messages have you received about treating yourself?

_____

_____

_____

_____

_____

_____

_____

_____

Learning to speak your truth is a valuable lesson. Whether you are advocating for your own needs or discussing an issue you feel passionately about, the world needs to hear you. Reflect on times when you have spoken up. How did you feel? How was your message received? If you haven't yet felt comfortable speaking up, what has gotten in the way and what are some things you'd like to say? Use the space below to jot down your thoughts.

_____

_____

_____

_____

_____

_____

_____

_____

_____

_____

_____

_____

_____

Step Out of Your Comfort Zone

How often do you step out of your comfort zone? Here's an opportunity. First, think of an activity you've wanted to try but haven't. For example, maybe it's ceramics or playing a new sport. After you've decided on an activity, gently challenge yourself by giving it a try. Then take some time to reflect: How did you feel before and after the activity? What did you learn about the experience? Note: If you're having trouble moving out of your comfort zone, ask for the support of a trusted friend or family member; we all need encouragement sometimes!

Fashion can be a fun form of creative expression. Take a look at your own unique style and how you present yourself to the world. Who has influenced your personal style? Is there an item of clothing or accessory that makes you feel most like yourself? If you were going to name your brand of personal style, what would you call it? When reflecting, feel free to use the space below to sketch, make lists, or jot down thoughts. Be as creative as you like!

_____

_____

_____

_____

_____

_____

_____

_____

_____

_____

_____

_____

_____

Reflect on your inner strength (a.k.a. resiliency). We all have it, but sometimes it goes by without the acknowledgment it deserves. Think about a time (or times) when life has felt hard. How did you handle it? What resources did you seek out? How did you care for yourself?

_____

_____

_____

_____

_____

_____

_____

_____

_____

_____

_____

_____

_____

_____

_____

Check-In Meditation

Often when others ask us how we're doing, we respond with an automatic "good" or "fine." This may be because we get so busy as we move through our days that we don't take the time to check in with ourselves. This is a meditation to gain insight into how you're *actually* feeling or doing so you can engage with others more authentically and care for yourself in the best way possible.

1. Find a space where you won't be disturbed for 10 to 15 minutes and sit upright in a comfortable position.

2. Begin by focusing on your feet. Observe any sensations you feel without judgment; just notice the sensations and emotions you experience.

3. Slowly move your focus upward, scanning your body as you go. Keep noting the sensations and emotions. Do any images come to mind? Any symbols or colors? As you reach the top of your head, know that your meditation is coming to an end.

4. When you have completed your meditation, slowly open your eyes and take in your surroundings.

Did you learn anything new about yourself? If you feel inspired, use the space below to create a sketch or drawing of what you experienced.

Everyone has a few pet peeves. What really gets under your skin? Set a timer for three to five minutes and free write, without censoring yourself, about what bugs you. When the timer goes off, it's time to pause and reflect. Do you notice any themes in what you've written? Did you learn anything new about yourself in this process?

_____

_____

_____

_____

_____

_____

_____

_____

_____

_____

_____

_____

_____

_____

The path to self-discovery is not a straight line. It's a zigzag. We move in and out of awareness: one step forward, three steps to the left, a baby step back, another leap forward.

—**ALICIA KEYS**, singer-songwriter and author

We live in a culture that often has us questioning the way we look. Let's explore our relationship to our physical selves. Take inventory of your emotions, and be honest with yourself. How do you feel about your body? How do you feel *in* your body? You may choose to reflect by using words or images to describe this relationship. Notice what emotions arise. Do you feel sad? Joyful? Angry? Empowered? All of the above? Use the space below to write or draw as much as you like.

Michael Jordan,
FORMER CHAMPIONSHIP-WINNING NBA PLAYER

Who says introverts can't excel in an extroverted world? Michael Jordan was one who proved how much introverts can accomplish. Considered by many to be the most skilled professional basketball player in history, Jordan was also known to be intensely introverted and at times reclusive, needing his privacy and alone time to retreat from the buzz of NBA fervor. Among Jordan's long list of achievements were 15 seasons in the NBA and winning six championships with the Chicago Bulls. He was named Final MVP in all six championships.

Self-Compassion Practice

Self-compassion goes hand in hand with healthy self-esteem. Here, we will practice a simple meditation in self-compassion.

1. First, find a space that feels peaceful to you and sit or lie down in a comfortable position. You may choose to practice this meditation before you go to sleep at night or when you wake up in the morning.

2. Next, put one or both hands over your heart and focus your attention on your heartbeat to help you focus on the present moment.

3. Take a deep breath in and extend kindness to yourself, however you perceive it. Release your breath slowly and mindfully, letting go any self-criticism you may have been holding on to.

4. Repeat this breathing practice three to five times. When you have completed your meditation, slowly open your eyes and take in your surroundings.

   How did this meditation feel? How might you incorporate it into your week?

_____

_____

_____

_____

_____

_____

When you look around your world, who inspires you? Is it a family member, a friend, or a teacher? Is it someone you've never met, like a writer, musician or fictional character? Think about and identify your role models. Write a list of people (real and fictional) who have inspired you. Make sure to include why they inspire you and, if it feels right, what you learn from them.

_____

_____

_____

_____

_____

_____

_____

_____

_____

_____

_____

_____

_____

_____

_____

Selfie Flex

Flex your selfie-taking skills to further explore and celebrate the unique aspects of yourself. First, stage a photo shoot! You can make this as simple or as elaborate as you like, choosing an environment that feels safe and comfortable for you. Next, snap a photo to represent an aspect of your identity. For example: Artistic Me, Student Me, Best Friend Me, Grumpy Me, etc. Last, share these photos with someone you feel supported by.

What was it like staging your own photo shoot? What did you notice about your feelings and self-talk? Were you comfortable sharing your selfies with others?

_____

_____

_____

_____

_____

Everyone messes up—that's how we learn. Often, though, we judge ourselves for the mistake instead of offering ourselves compassion, the way we would a friend. Reflect on a time when you made a mistake and were not able to offer yourself compassion. What could you say to yourself differently and more compassionately?

_____

_____

_____

_____

_____

_____

_____

_____

_____

_____

_____

_____

_____

_____

Know Your Boundaries

Knowing our own physical boundaries helps us take better care of ourselves. Each person's boundaries are different, so to understand your boundaries, set aside time to spend with family or friends. You can engage in any activity, but pay special attention to how you feel in close proximity to people you know well. Are you comfortable with someone sitting right next to you? Walking past you? Are you comfortable with physical touch? What feels like a comfortable distance? Did you learn something surprising about your boundaries?

_____

_____

_____

_____

_____

Teen activist Greta Thunberg has made significant impacts in climate change activism. Teen activist Desmond Napoles, well-known through stage name Desmond is Amazing, has raised their voice for LGBTQ+ youth representation. What social issues are you passionate about? Make a list of the issues that concern you locally, nationally, and globally. Are you inspired to take action?

_____

_____

_____

_____

_____

_____

_____

_____

_____

_____

_____

_____

Tell Me What You See

Sometimes it's hard for us to see our own strengths, and it can be helpful to ask for feedback. Reach out to one to three people you feel supported by and who know you well. Ask them to reflect on five of your greatest strengths with you. If you feel inspired, you can do the same for them. I bet you'll be surprised at how people are eager to share their positive impressions of you!

How did you feel about asking for feedback? What feelings came up when you received the feedback? Did anything surprise you?

_____

_____

_____

_____

_____

Celebrate who you are by writing a love letter to yourself! Don't hold back. This is your opportunity to love up on yourself in a way that feels real and nourishing. Feel free to include reflections on your strengths, achievements, quirks, and resilience.

_____

_____

_____

_____

_____

_____

_____

_____

_____

_____

_____

_____

section 3
The Social You

While introverts tend to need their quiet time and prefer small groups to large ones, relationships are just as important to us as they are to anyone else. On this leg of our journey, we'll take a closer look at our relationships, communities, social preferences, and communication styles as another step in getting to know ourselves better and gaining skills and insights for more fulfilling social interactions.

Being different means you make the difference.

–JUSTIN TIMBERLAKE, singer and actor

Think about a social interaction when you felt relaxed and like you could be your most authentic self. Were you with friends or family? Was the space quiet or busy? Were you outside or inside? Write down the details of the event and how you felt. What were the qualities that made you feel most at ease?

_____

_____

_____

_____

_____

_____

_____

_____

_____

_____

_____

_____

_____

_____

Getting Grounded (When You're Not)

It's common for introverts to feel overwhelmed in social situations. Sounds, colors, even scents can feel like too much. Times like these are an excellent opportunity to practice basic mindfulness skills.

1. First, gently turn your attention away from the outer world and toward your inner world.

2. Notice the thoughts and feelings that come up for you in the moment.

3. Without judgment, practice naming these thoughts in a way that feels useful. Some examples may be "anxious thought" or "overwhelmed." Some people choose to be more playful by labeling these types of thoughts with a person's name, for example.

   Using this practice can help create distance between you and the thoughts and feelings you experience. What did you notice?

   _____

   _____

   _____

Even the most solid relationships with friends and family experience turbulence from time to time. We disagree or hurt each other's feelings. When conflict arises, how do you handle it? Is your tendency to retreat, or do you want to talk about it right away? Use this space to reflect on your communication style during conflict. Is there anything you would change? This is also a great time to take note of how your communication style compares to those close to you. For example, do you like to talk things out right away, while your best friend needs time and space?

_____

_____

_____

_____

_____

_____

_____

_____

_____

_____

_____

_____

Barack Obama,
FORMER PRESIDENT OF THE UNITED STATES

Barack Obama was the 44th president of the United States and made history as the first Black, biracial president. Unlike his predecessor, President Bill Clinton, who was known for his gregarious nature, President Obama was, by definition, an introvert. He led with quiet confidence and was often viewed as stoic. Prior to the end of his term as president, Obama shared his daily rituals with the *New York Times*. Among these rituals were long hours spent in solitude every evening after dinner with his family. The time was said to have been for introspection, productivity, and recharging. Obama is a clear example of how even the quietest among us can harness their introversion and rise to the highest ranks.

Most of us belong to one or more communities. This affiliation could be based on our interests, address, school, or spiritual path. Take a moment to reflect on what affiliations you have in your life and how they came to be. Did you choose these communities, or were they based on family decisions or location? What communities would you want to be part of and why?

_____

_____

_____

_____

_____

_____

_____

_____

_____

_____

_____

_____

_____

Express Your Needs

It can be hard to express ourselves when we feel upset, but talking through difficulties can make relationships stronger. In this activity, we'll practice basic nonviolent communication skills (NVC) with a trusted person in our lives. NVC is a model for communication rooted in empathy and connection.

1. First, identify your feelings and express them with an "I feel" statement, such as *I feel frustrated because I feel unheard.*

2. Next, identify and express your needs, such as *I need to know you're listening to me.*

3. Last, make a request to the other person based on your feelings and needs. What is the action you'd like them to take? You could say, *Please make eye contact when we're speaking so I know you're paying attention.*

   Note that the other person then gets to decide if they can fulfill the request. By sharing your feelings, needs, and requests, you are opening up lines of communication for a more supportive dynamic.

It's common to have a love-hate relationship with social media. After all, it can be a powerful tool for staying connected with others, and yet sometimes we find ourselves comparing ourselves and our lives to those of others. Reflect on your relationship to social media by creating a pros-and-cons list about using social media. Now compare which list is longer. Did any of your answers surprise you? What keeps you motivated to use social media?

_____

_____

_____

_____

_____

_____

_____

_____

_____

_____

_____

_____

_____

Most of us have experienced at least one awkward social moment in our lives, like the time we couldn't find the words or said the wrong thing. Reflect on a time when things didn't go the way you would have wanted them to. What happened, and how did you get through it? If you felt overwhelmed by the experience, what would you do differently next time to care for yourself?

_____

_____

_____

_____

_____

_____

_____

_____

_____

_____

_____

_____

_____

_____

_____

You draw your own box.
You introduce yourself as
who you are . . .
You create the identity
you want for yourself.

—**MEGHAN MARKLE**, Duchess of Sussex and former actress

Everyone experiences loss in their relationships, whether it's a friend, family member, pet, or someone else they've felt close to. The experience can weigh heavy in our hearts, and yet expressing those feelings can be healing. Try to reflect on an experience of loss by either writing down your memory of the experience or drafting a letter to the person you lost. How has this experience influenced how you connect with others?

_____

_____

_____

_____

_____

_____

_____

_____

_____

_____

_____

_____

_____

Quiet Your Inner Critic

It's common for our inner critic to get loud in social situations. They may spend their time fueling doubts and insecurities, but you don't have to let them run the show! An easy strategy for managing your inner critic is by responding with kindness. You don't have to wait until your next social engagement to practice. Today, as you're moving through your day and you notice doubts or insecurities popping up, practice offering words of kindness to yourself. For example, if your inner critic is saying something like "You'll never be good enough," you may consider responding with "I do the best I can every day, and that is enough."

What did you notice about your inner critic's messages? Were they familiar or new? How did you feel responding with kind sentiments? Did it come easily, or was it challenging?

_____

_____

_____

_____

_____

_____

_____

_____

If thinking about your inner critic is challenging, keep going! It can take some time to rein in our inner critic, but it's possible.

Family comes in different constellations. For some, family is biological; for others, family comprises chosen folks in our lives. Often, it's a mix of both. Take a moment to consider how you define family and whom you include as your own. If you feel inspired, you may use the space below to draw a family tree, however you imagine it to be. What feelings come up when you think about the concept of family?

Relationship Reflection

How do you envision healthy relationships? What colors, shapes, and symbols come to mind? Create a sculpture from found objects to represent your view of healthy connection. Found objects can be things located in your home or in nature. Outside, these may include flowers, fallen bark or branches from trees, or rocks. Inside, you may find old magazines or pictures, jewelry, or dishes (make sure you get permission if the objects don't belong to you!). You can either arrange these objects together temporarily to create a sculpture and take a photo or use glue or tape to hold them together to keep for longer. What did you notice about this process? What would you title your artwork?

_____

_____

_____

_____

_____

Sometimes we meet someone and click with them immediately. Other times, the connection builds slowly. Think of someone you consider to be a best friend or very close friend. What qualities does that relationship have? What was your first impression of them? How has that relationship evolved, and how have each of you nourished the connection?

_____

_____

_____

_____

_____

_____

_____

_____

_____

_____

_____

_____

_____

_____

Manage FOMO

Let's talk about the fear of missing out. It's an understandable experience at times. Yet if it happens too frequently, it can hold us hostage and keep us glued to social media instead of living our lives. Here's a challenge: Try to take a break from social media for one to three days. Notice how you felt at the beginning, middle, and end of your break. What feelings came up? How did you fill your time? Do you see a benefit to repeating a break like this?

_____

_____

_____

_____

_____

A bias is a judgment for or against something or someone based on your own perception. Some common biases are based on race, gender identity, ability, and sexual orientation. Often we don't even realize we have these biases until we are confronted with them or take time to examine them. Although it can be difficult to acknowledge our own biases without becoming defensive, it is important to do so honestly. First, think about a time when you may have experienced bias. What happened in that incident, and how did it make you feel? Did you receive support? Next, take an honest look at your own biases. Do you find yourself judging specific groups or certain personality traits? Reflect on any thoughts or feelings that arise on the subject of bias.

_____

_____

_____

_____

_____

_____

_____

_____

_____

_____

_____

_____

_____

_____

_____

_____

_____

_____

_____

_____

_____

_____

_____

_____

_____

_____

_____

_____

_____

_____

_____

Let's pretend your life is a movie and you, of course, are the main character. Now zoom out for a moment: Who is in the supporting cast? Use this space to be as creative as you like as you imagine your autobiography on screen. What relationships would be important to feature, and who would play the roles?

_____

_____

_____

_____

_____

_____

_____

_____

_____

_____

_____

_____

_____

_____

_____

Plan Your Perfect Gathering

How often do you initiate social plans? Let's practice organizing activities that suit your introverted nature. First, check in with yourself and consider what you feel like doing today. Maybe it's something outdoors, like having a picnic at a nearby park with a family member, going to a movie with friends, or organizing a sleepover. Try choosing an activity that will support connection between you and those you care about. Next, send invitations with a proposed date and time. If this is new to you, you may ask for additional support from a caregiver or trusted adult.

How did you feel taking an organizer role? What went particularly well about this experience? If there were any changes you'd make, what would you do differently next time?

_____

_____

_____

_____

_____

Think back to a time you disagreed with an authority figure, such as a teacher or another adult. What happened that prompted the disagreement, and how did you respond? Did you choose to engage and show your displeasure with words or actions, or did you choose to hold your feelings inside? Take a moment to reflect on this dynamic. Looking back, would you change anything about the interaction?

_____

_____

_____

_____

_____

_____

_____

_____

_____

_____

_____

_____

_____

Share Your Feelings

Are you someone who holds your feelings close and hesitates to share them? Ease out of your comfort zone a bit and practice being vulnerable with a trusted person in your life. Think about a feeling, thought, or experience you've been keeping to yourself that you'd truly like to share. Keep in mind this does not need to be a difficult thing to share; it can be a celebration of a success or an appreciation you have for someone else. You may choose to share in conversation, through writing, or even by sending a text.

How did it feel to share something you would normally keep to yourself? What did you notice in the process?

_____

_____

_____

_____

_____

Give and Take

While we're gaining skills in asking for what we need in relationships, it's also important to be mindful of what we bring to our relationships. Today, pay attention to how you can support those around you. The next time you are talking with a friend or family member, consider asking them how you can offer help or support. Some examples may include listening, helping out with chores, or offering words of encouragement. Remember to celebrate the achievements and joyful moments of those closest to you just as much as you support them when they are going through a challenge.

Did you know one of the easiest (and most fun) ways to navigate new social situations is to become skilled at asking questions? Question asking takes the pressure off those of us who feel like we have to say the right thing and gives us the opportunity to learn more about others. When you meet a new person, what are the things you want to know about them? Practice asking questions for real-life social situations. As you ask questions, come from a place of authenticity and curiosity, and see where this leads you!

_____

_____

_____

_____

_____

_____

_____

_____

_____

_____

_____

_____

Often when we argue with a friend, it's difficult to understand where they're coming from. Think back to a conflict you've had with someone you care about. Write what happened in detail. Now step into their shoes. How do you imagine they experienced the argument? How does this insight change your view of what happened?

_____

_____

_____

_____

_____

_____

_____

_____

_____

_____

_____

_____

_____

_____

Walk in My Shoes

One way to connect with others is through the practice of empathy. To empathize means to be able to understand someone else's feelings or experiences. It is a social skill that helps deepen our relationships. Let's practice empathizing with others. The next time you're having a one-on-one conversation with someone, try this activity:

1. First, visualize stepping into their shoes and take a look around. What do you imagine their perspective to be?

2. Now, focus on listening to the other person without judgment as they speak.

3. Note what emotions they share and think of a time when you have felt that emotion.

4. When the other person is done speaking, share that you, too, have experienced the same emotion. If it feels appropriate, ask how and if you can help.

Do you find empathizing comes easily, or does it take practice? Do you feel others in your life empathize with you? How does it make you feel?

_____

_____

_____

_____

_____

_____

As we grow, it's natural for our relationships to change or end and new relationships to form. Take a moment to reflect on how your relationships have changed (or stayed the same) from early childhood until now. Are you friends with the same people? Have you outgrown some relationships? If so, how did you know?

_____

_____

_____

_____

_____

_____

_____

_____

_____

_____

_____

_____

_____

_____

_____

Social media helps us stay connected with people we already know and can help us form new connections with people we might otherwise never meet. Think about how you present yourself on social media versus in person. Do you notice any differences? Are you bolder in one venue than the other? Are there any changes you would make based on what you've discovered?

_____

_____

_____

_____

_____

_____

_____

_____

_____

_____

_____

_____

_____

_____

A Day of Yes!

Television producer and writer Shonda Rhimes wrote an entire book called *Year of Yes* about stepping out of her comfort zone as an introvert. Let's follow her lead and try a Day of Yes. Set aside one day where you say yes to activities or opportunities that you might typically say no to because they are outside your comfort zone. Go at your own pace here and use your best judgment in choosing your yeses!

Did you love or hate some of these new activities? What did you learn?

_____

_____

_____

_____

_____

Choose people who lift you up.

—**MICHELLE OBAMA**, former First Lady of the United States

section 4
The Future You

Welcome to section 4 of this journal, your final leg of this journey. In this section, we'll take some time to imagine, explore, and unpack our hopes, dreams, and questions about our future selves. There's no pressure here to have a clear vision of what life may look like after high school—or in 20 years, for that matter! The prompts and exercises in this section are intended to support your curiosity and imagination only.

He's a wallflower . . .
You see things. You keep
quiet about them.
And you understand.

—**STEPHEN CHBOSKY**, author of
The Perks of Being a Wallflower

What images, feelings, and thoughts arise when you think of the future? How do you feel in your body—tense or calm? Let your mind wander and see where it brings you. You may find yourself feeling excited, anxious, curious, or a mixture of many emotions. Use this space to write about your experience without judgment.

_____

_____

_____

_____

_____

_____

_____

_____

_____

_____

_____

_____

_____

_____

Our journeys are often long and winding. Think about your journey so far. Where have you come from? What are the most important lessons you've learned, and what wisdom would you offer others based on the experiences you've had? Write your thoughts down here.

_____

_____

_____

_____

_____

_____

_____

_____

_____

_____

_____

_____

_____

_____

Life Events Passport

We each experience key events in our lives that help shape us and inform the next part of our journey. Sometimes these are big events like graduation or a marriage; other times, the events may be quieter. For this activity, create a Life Events Passport to illustrate the events you are looking forward to. To make the passport, take five 8½-by-11-inch sheets of paper, cut them in half along the short side, and fold the stack together to create a booklet. You can staple the center or use glue. Then, using markers, collage, or any medium you like, create pages to represent and celebrate these life events.

Sarah Corbett, SOCIAL ACTIVIST

Sarah Corbett has found a way to follow her calling as a social justice and environmental activist while honoring her "extremely introverted" nature. Corbett, who was raised in the United Kingdom by politically active parents, was engaged in traditional activism, such as protests and rallies, starting at the age of three. But despite her passion for social issues, Corbett became burned out by these types of actions. Then she discovered the work of American writer and crafter Betsy Greer, who was working at the intersection of crafting and activism and coined the term "craftivism." This form of social action is described as quiet, reflective, gentle protest and takes many forms. In 2009, Corbett formed the Craftivist Collective, an international network of activists committed to using craft as a way to raise consciousness about social issues.

Introverts often lean toward careers that allow for introspection and quiet environments. When you think about future careers, what do you imagine? Perhaps you see yourself as someone who creates things or helps others. Maybe you'll own a business or be a full-time parent or caregiver. Create a list of three to five professions you may be interested in, and write about why you chose them.

_____

_____

_____

_____

_____

_____

_____

_____

_____

_____

_____

_____

_____

_____

Do you believe we create our own paths or that a higher power chooses for us? Perhaps you believe both or neither. Reflect on your belief system when it comes to the future. If you're not sure, consider making a list of questions that come up.

_____

_____

_____

_____

_____

_____

_____

_____

_____

_____

_____

_____

_____

_____

_____

_____

Chasing Your Dream

Our dreams can sometimes feel out of reach because we don't know where to get started. Pick one goal or dream you have for the future and identify another person who has already achieved a similar one. This may be someone you already know, such as an older peer or adult, or someone you've researched and would be interested in talking to, like a community member or local policy maker. Contact them in a way that feels comfortable for you, whether by phone or email, and ask them how they got started. You may choose to ask what obstacles they faced, if there is any guidance they may offer as you walk the same path, or any other questions that come to mind. Did you learn anything unexpected?

Imagine yourself during the next five years of your life. What do you see yourself doing after high school? Would you want to live on your own or with others? What would you like your social life to involve, and what activities would you engage in to care for yourself? Keeping in mind your unique wants and needs, take some time now to jot down your goals for the next five years. They can be as broad or specific as you like.

_____

_____

_____

_____

_____

_____

_____

_____

_____

_____

_____

_____

_____

I'm realizing now . . .
that there's a lot of
strength in showing
people that everything
is not always daisies
every single minute of
every single day.

—LANA CONDOR, actress

Do you have wanderlust—a craving to see the world, meet new people, and explore new cultures? If so, reflect on where you'd like to travel and why. Where are you pulled to? If you are eager to travel but hesitant, what holds you back, and how can you overcome your fear?

_____

_____

_____

_____

_____

_____

_____

_____

_____

_____

_____

_____

_____

_____

Your Future Self

Do you ever wonder who you will turn out to be?

1. Find a quiet space and close your eyes.

2. Let your mind wander to a future version of yourself. You may find yourself at 30 or 80 years old!

3. How does your future self feel physically and emotionally? What is your personal style like? What activities do you enjoy? What kind of job or school are you involved in?

4. Now create an "I Am" poem for your future self. In the space below, begin each line with *I am* ____ and fill in the blank with whatever comes to mind.

_____

_____

_____

_____

_____

_____

_____

When you think about the future, what worries, if any, arise about yourself or the world around you? This can be specific to personal concerns or to social issues. Try not to censor yourself here, but just be open to what arises.

_____

_____

_____

_____

_____

_____

_____

_____

_____

_____

_____

_____

_____

_____

Imagine it's the first day of the fall semester after you've graduated high school, and you've been asked to return to deliver a speech to the incoming freshman class. You're excited to share the wisdom you've accumulated over the past four years. What advice would you give to the incoming freshman class? What do you wish you knew when you were starting high school? What challenges did you face, and how did you navigate them? Write a speech or monologue here about what you would say.

_____

_____

_____

_____

_____

_____

_____

_____

_____

_____

_____

_____

_____

Zendaya, ACTRESS

Now in her mid-20s, actress and model Zendaya has been active in the entertainment industry since she was a young child. Zendaya, who is a self-identified introvert, described herself as a shy kid, so much so that her parents educated themselves in how to best support her. Zendaya has said that finding her passion in theater and the arts helped her feel more at ease and come out of her shell; however, learning to navigate extroverted Hollywood was challenging. Noting that she felt bullied at times from other child actors, Zendaya said she got through it by staying true to herself and perhaps even relying on her introverted nature as a strength. "I'd literally sit there before auditions with my headphones on, listening to Michael Jackson," she's said. Zendaya's story illustrates how even the most introverted among us can succeed in extrovert-dominated fields.

Mindful Eating

Thinking about the future may be exciting and sometimes overwhelming. This is to be expected given just how much there is to consider! Mindfulness is a helpful tool to calm our busy minds by focusing on the here and now. Finding new ways to incorporate mindfulness into your daily life doesn't have to be difficult or time-consuming. In fact, it can be . . . tasty. Here's how it works:

1. Choose a food that you really enjoy!

2. Take a piece of the food, either in your hand or on a utensil, and look at it closely. Note the colors, textures, and smells.

3. Next, take a small bite and chew with all your attention on the experience. What is the texture? What is the flavor? What did you notice? You may try this with your eyes open or closed.

What did you observe about this experience of eating? How did the food taste? How does it differ from when you're eating and talking to others or your attention is elsewhere?

_____

_____

_____

_____

_____

_____

_____

Often we're told to be realistic about our goals for the future, but I'm inviting you to cast that notion aside for a moment and tap into your wildest dreams. If anything was possible and nothing was holding you back, what would you like your future to look like? Why did you choose this version of the future? What hurdles are in the way, and can anything be done to jump them?

_____

_____

_____

_____

_____

_____

_____

_____

_____

_____

_____

_____

_____

_____

Preparing to Launch

As we continue to grow into adulthood, we learn new life skills so that we can take care of ourselves. Pause and consider what areas you feel you need to learn more about. Your list may look very different, whether you are 13 or 18 years old. That's to be expected.

Here are some examples to get you started:

- Driving a car or taking public transportation
- Cooking meals
- Budgeting money
- Paying bills
- Completing job applications
- Looking for apartments

Use this space to jot down questions or ideas you have. What is it like for you to think about "adulting"? After you've made your list, is there a trusted mentor, parent, or guardian you can ask for help in learning these new skills?

_____

_____

_____

_____

_____

_____

_____

Everyone has unique gifts they bring to the world. When you think about your future self, what do you imagine will be your most meaningful contribution? For some, it may be tied to a profession or volunteer work. For others, it may be connected to their creativity or family. The sky's the limit here. What will you give to the world?

_____

_____

_____

_____

_____

_____

_____

_____

_____

_____

_____

_____

_____

_____

_____

Imagine yourself in the future coming home from a big social gathering and needing some time to recharge. What would your dream home look like? Use the space below to write or sketch a representation of your personal sanctuary. Is it in the city or the mountains? Is it a posh mansion or an industrial loft? What colors and textures do you see?

Vision Walk

Are you unsure about a future goal or plan? It happens to all of us, and yet sometimes we actually already have the answers we seek! We just have to get out of our own way to access them. Take a vision walk to tap into your own wisdom.

1. First, identify a question you are grappling with. Maybe you have a big decision to make or you need clarity on a bigger vision.

2. Set aside time to go walking outside for 30 to 60 minutes. This time can be spent in nature or an urban setting. Any place will work just fine. As you start out, set the intention of being open and curious to your process. Try to avoid listening to music during this time.

3. As you walk, be mindful of where your attention goes. What do you notice in your surroundings? What do you hear or see? What are you thinking about?

4. When you arrive back home, jot down some notes about what you noticed.

Sometimes there is an immediate connection made between something we witnessed and the questions we were trying to answer, but it's not always immediate. If you're still struggling to find your answer, you may choose to revisit your notes in the upcoming weeks to see whether you have gained any new perspectives.

_____

_____

_____

Often our most challenging experiences are our greatest teachers. When you think of your life so far, what have been some of those most difficult lessons you've learned? If given the option, would you change how things played out?

_____

_____

_____

_____

_____

_____

_____

_____

_____

_____

_____

_____

_____

_____

Body Scan Meditation

Just like the caterpillar in its chrysalis, the teen years are full of growth and transformation. It's such an exciting period that can bring up a whirlwind of emotion. Take a moment to check in with yourself through a body scan meditation to see how you're feeling on your journey.

1. Begin by sitting or lying down in a quiet and comfortable space.

2. Then bring your attention to your feet and notice any sensations or feelings that arise. Take a deep breath and release.

3. Slowly move your attention up through your body, simply noticing and breathing as you did in step 2, until you reach the top of your head.

    What did you notice as you were practicing the body scan? Did any emotions arise? Did you gain any new insights into your experience?

_____

_____

_____

_____

_____

_____

On any given day, we visit the past and plan for the future while trying to stay present in our current lives. Where do you find your mind goes most often? In what realm are you most comfortable or most anxious? Where would you like to be and why?

_____

_____

_____

_____

_____

_____

_____

_____

_____

_____

_____

_____

_____

_____

_____

Inspiration Grab Bag

Sometimes we need a little extra inspiration. For this project, we're going to make an Inspiration Grab Bag. First, research a minimum of 15 to 25 inspirational quotes that resonate with you and write them down on a separate sheet of paper. The more quotes you have the better. These quotes may be from books, songs, poems, celebrities, or people you know and respect. Cut the quotes into strips of paper and fold them, putting them inside a paper bag, a box, or any other container that you have handy. On days when you're feeling like you need positive messages, reach in and see what wisdom is at your fingertips!

Imagine yourself as an elderly person. You have lived a full and rewarding life. What wisdom do you have to share with your current self? Now, write a letter from your future self to your current self.

_____

_____

_____

_____

_____

_____

_____

_____

_____

_____

_____

_____

_____

_____

_____

_____

Letting Go Ritual

Consider what it's time to let go of. You'll need two sheets of paper. On one sheet of paper, draw an outline of a suitcase. On the other sheet, draw a compost bin. You can also find and print images off the internet instead of drawing or simply draw two circles that represent each object—there's no wrong way to do this! In the suitcase, write down all the helpful feelings, memories, and lessons you've learned thus far that you want to take with you on your journey. In the compost bin, write down all the feelings, memories, and experiences that no longer serve you. When you're finished, create a simple ritual to "recycle the compost." You may choose to tear up the paper, put it someplace tucked away, or put it in a bowl of water until the paper disintegrates. Make sure to set aside time to reflect. What feelings came up in this process?

Affirmations are positive phrases or messages that support you in your day-to-day life. Sometimes they are used to help you keep a positive mindset or to support you in achieving a goal. Write down some affirmations that support your vision of your future self. An example might be "I am growing into the best version of myself." Another might be "I am trusting my journey." Write down statements that are authentic and truly resonate with you.

_____

_____

_____

_____

_____

_____

_____

_____

_____

_____

_____

_____

Vision Share

It can feel supportive to share our visions and dreams with a trusted friend. Pick someone close to you and set a date to share your vision of the future with them. Invite them to do the same. What feelings arose for you in this process? How can you support each other as you move closer to your respective goals?

_____

_____

_____

_____

_____

_____

_____

_____

_____

_____

_____

_____

_____

Step out of the history
that is holding you back.
Step into the new story
you are willing to create.

—**OPRAH WINFREY**, media mogul and philanthropist

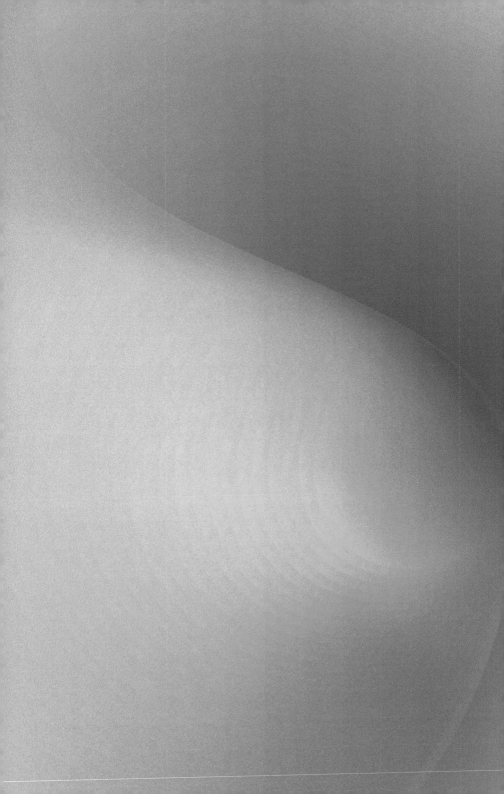

Resources

Books

Embracing the Awkward: A Guide for Teens to Succeed at School, Life, and Relationships by Joshua Rodriguez
A great skills-based book to help you expand your toolkit for navigating your teen years. This book covers topics ranging from mindfulness to creating healthy relationships.

Nonviolent Communication: A Language of Life by Marshall B. Rosenberg
If you're interested in learning more about nonviolent communication skills (NVC), this book is a great place to start. Here you'll learn skills to practice expressing yourself authentically.

The Perks of Being a Wallflower by Stephen Chbosky
A novel that nicely depicts the teen experience as a whole, as well as characters that are more introverted. There's a movie version, too!

Quiet: The Power of Introverts in a World That Can't Stop Talking by Susan Cain
Susan Cain is an expert on introversion and has written two books on the subject. *Quiet* is recommended for ages 15 and up.

Quiet Power: The Secret Strengths of Introverted Kids by Susan Cain
This is the second book by Susan Cain, and it's recommended for ages 10 to 15.

Blogs and Websites

Craftivist Collective
Craftivist-Collective.com
As featured in an anecdote in section 4 (see page 102), the *Craftivist Collective* is a social activism hub for introverts.

Introvert, Dear
IntrovertDear.com
Introvert, Dear is an award-winning blog about all things introverted, including tips and tricks for navigating an extroverted world. It features numerous writers from diverse backgrounds.

The Introvert's Corner
PsychologyToday.com/us/blog/the-introverts-corner
The Introvert's Corner is another blog written by Dallas-based writer Sophia Dembling. The blog normalizes the introvert's desire for a "quiet life."

Apps

Calm
Calm.com
If you're interested in continuing or expanding your mindfulness and meditation practices, Calm offers a wide array of directive and non-directive meditations, as well as soothing music and nature sounds if you just need a break from the buzz of daily life.

Daylio
Daylio.net
A journal app, diary, and mood tracker, this app works a bit differently from others. You choose from a list of moods and activities to track your day-to-day experience. Daylio computes your entries and provides stats and charts, giving you a different way to understand your experiences.

Five Minute Journal
IntelligentChange.com/products/five-minute-journal-app
A journal app that provides daily prompts to reflect on gratitude. You're also able to upload photos and videos, as well as create your own prompts for reflection.

Headspace
Headspace.com
Similar to Calm, this is another app that will guide you through continuing or expanding your mindfulness and meditation practices.

Jour
Jour.com
With an emphasis on self-care, this guided journaling app uses prompts to help you reflect on your feelings, thoughts, and behaviors.

References

Brown, August. "Fast-Rising Artist Billie Eilish Shows Pop's Future Has Arrived." *Los Angeles Times*. March 7, 2018. latimes.com /entertainment/music/la-et-ms-billie-eilish-20180301 -story.html.

Brown, Damon. "The Leader of the Free World Is an Introvert. Here's How Obama Leads." *Inc.* July 5, 2016. inc.com/damon-brown /the-leader-of-the-free-world-is-an-introvert.html.

Butler, Octavia E. *Parable of the Sower*. New York: Grand Central Publishing, 1993.

Cain, Susan. *Quiet: The Power of Introverts in a World That Can't Stop Talking*. New York: Crown Publishing Group, 2013.

Carroll, Lewis. *Alice's Adventures in Wonderland*. Sweden: Wise-house Classics, 2016.

Chbosky, Stephen. *The Perks of Being a Wallflower*. New York: Simon & Schuster, 2012.

Cole, Samantha. "7 Famous Leaders Who Prove Introverts Can Be Wildly Successful." *Fast Company*. June 18, 2014. fastcompany.com/3032028/7-famous-leaders-who-prove-introverts-can-be-wildly-successful.

Craftivist Collective. "Our Story." Craftivist-Collective.com. Accessed April 12, 2021. craftivist-collective.com/our-story.

Dinh, James. "Justin Timberlake Promotes Inclusion during Song of the Year Acceptance Speech at #iHeartAwards." March 5, 2017. iheart.com/content/2017-03-05-justin-timberlake-reps-for -inclusion-during-song-of-the-year-acceptance-speech-at -iheartawards.

Dodero, Camille. "Billboard Women in Music 'Rule Breaker' Alessia Cara: 'Having to Work Harder Makes Me Feel Like Girls Are Stronger.'" *Billboard*. December 10, 2016. billboard.com/articles /news/women-in-music/7597306/billboard-women-in-music -rule-breaker-alessia-cara.

Ferndandez, Celia. "21 Frida Kahlo Quotes as Evocative as Her Paintings." Oprah Daily. March 15, 2019. oprahdaily.com/life /relationships-love/g26840075/frida-kahlo-quotes.

"Frida Kahlo Biography." FridaKahlo.org. Accessed April 14, 2021. fridakahlo.org/frida-kahlo-biography.jsp.

Keys, Alicia. *More Myself: A Journey*. New York: Flatiron Books, 2020.

Markle, Meghan. "I'm More Than an Other." *Elle UK*. Last updated March 8, 2020. elle.com/uk/life-and-culture/news/a26855 /more-than-an-other.

Muir, David. *Nightline* Interview: Michelle Obama. *ABC News*. June 23, 2011. abcnews.go.com/nightline/video/obama-michelle -daughters-children-kids-president-first-lady-13919884.

NBA History. "Legends Profile: Michael Jordan." NBA.org. Accessed April 23, 2021. NBA.com/history/legends/profiles /michael-jordan.

Parks, Rosa, and Gregory J. Reed. *Quiet Strength*. Grand Rapids, Michigan: Zondervan, 1994.

Parton, Dolly. April 8, 2015. 12:40 p.m. twitter.com/dollyparton /status/585890099583397888.

Perkins, Nichole. "Lana Condor Says Goodbye to Lara Jean." *SELF*. February 2, 2021. self.com/story/lana-condor.

The Power of Vulnerability. Directed by Katy Davis. London: RSA Shorts, 2013.

Raz, Guy. "Sarah Corbett: How Can Introverts Be Activists Too?" Ted Radio Hour. NPR/KQED. April 12, 2019. npr.org/transcripts /711196501.

Rhimes, Shonda. *A Year of Yes: How to Dance It Out, Stand in the Sun, and Be Your Own Person*. New York: Simon & Schuster, 2015.

Robinson, Lisa. "Yes, Lorde's New Songs are Definitely about Her Personal Life." *Vanity Fair*. June 15, 2017. vanityfair.com /style/2017/06/lorde-melodrama-album.

Rosenberg, Marshall B. *Nonviolent Communication: A Language of Life*. 3rd ed. Encinitas, California: Puddle Dancer Press, 2015.

Rumi. *The Forbidden Rumi: The Suppressed Poems of Rumi on Love, Heresy, and Intoxication*. Rochester, Vermont: Inner Traditions, 2006.

Schumer, Amy. *The Girl with the Lower Back Tattoo*. New York: Gallery Books, 2016.

Shear, Michael D. "Obama After Dark: The Precious Hours Alone."
The New York Times. July 2, 2016. nytimes.com/2016/07/03
/us/politics/obama-after-dark-the-precious-hours-alone.html.

Tomey, Alyssa. "Zendaya Covers *Teen Vogue*, Explains Why She Has
No Desire to Ditch Disney . . . Yet." E! Online. January 6, 2015.
eonline.com/news/611571/zendaya-covers-teen-vogue
-explains-why-she-has-no-desire-to-ditch-disney-yet.

Wilding, Melody. "The Quiet Strength of the Ambitious Introvert."
Forbes. September 9, 2019. Forbes.com/sites/melody
wilding/2019/09/09/the-quiet-strength-of-the-ambitious
--introvert.

Winfrey, Oprah. *What I Know for Sure.* New York: Flatiron
Books, 2014.

Acknowledgments

This project is the culmination of more than a decade of working with youth in creative collaboration. I want to thank my professors and colleagues at the California Institute of Integral Studies Expressive Arts Therapy program, where my formal training began. Thanks to my clinical supervisors and co-therapists who encouraged my use of the arts and out-of-the-box interventions in my clinical work, and all my clients and their families for the honor of working with them in the spirit of co-exploration. Lastly, I want to thank my editor, Nora Spiegel, and Callisto Media for their vision in publishing this book, as well as my mother (who gifted me my first journal) and my father for his unyielding support. Thank you!

About the Author

Jessika Fruchter, LMFT, is a licensed marriage and family therapist based in the San Francisco Bay Area of California. She holds a master's degree in counseling psychology and expressive arts therapy from the California Institute of Integral Studies.

Jessika has been working with youth for more than a decade in school and community settings, foster care, and the juvenile justice system. In her private practice, Jessika specializes in supporting self-identified women and teen girls with issues of anxiety, stress, and trauma.

Originally from New York, Jessika is also a writer, artist, teacher, and activist, trying to navigate this precious life with humor, grace, humility, and personal style the best she can. You can learn more about Jessika's work at JessikaFruchterMFT.com, or join her on Instagram at @bay_area_feminist_therapist.